THE RIGHT TO HOUSING

A BLUEPRINT FOR

HOUSING THE NATION

D1716586

Institute for Policy Studies
Working Group on Housing
with Dick Cluster

This is a booklet version of A Progressive Housing Program for America, a document drafted, over a three-year period, by the IPS Working Group on Housing. Dick Cluster was engaged by the Working Group to assume primary responsibility for writing the booklet, with substantial assistance from Emily Achtenberg and Michael Stone. Chester Hartman provided final editorial assistance and supervised the production process, with additional contributions by Peter Dreier. Richard Appelbaum had primary responsibility for putting the original Program into written form, Carole Norris for the early organization of the Working Group and its funding.

Other members of the Working Group are: John Atlas, Robert Goodman, Jacqueline Leavitt, Daniel Lindheim, Peter Marcuse, Christine Minnehan, Michael Rawson, Florence Roisman, and Joel Rubenzahl. Sasha Natapoff assisted in the editing and production.

The Working Group was funded by grants from the Shalan Foundation, the Sunflower Foundation, and the Seed Fund, and loans from Community Economics, Inc. and the Community for Creative Non-Violence.

Design and production by Chip Cliffe.

This booklet is available from: Community Economics, Inc., 1904 Franklin Street #900, Oakland, CA 94612. Individual copies are $5.00 plus $2.00 postage and handling. Substantial discounts are available for bulk orders.

The IPS Working Group on Housing may be contacted through Chester Hartman, IPS, 1601 Connecticut Avenue N.W., Washington, DC 20009.

ISBN: 0-89758-046-X

94
autumn press

Contents

CHAPTER 1

The Housing Problem..1

   1. A Housing Crisis 2

   2. Causes: The Private Housing Sector 10

   3. Causes: Government Actions 15

CHAPTER 2

A Progressive Housing Program for America 23

   1. Goals 24

   2. Preserving Affordable Rental Housing 31

   3. Promoting Affordable Homeownership 38

   4. Protecting Government-Assisted Housing 45

   5. Producing and Financing Affordable Housing......................52

   6. Conclusion 59

CHAPTER 3

First-Year Program Costs 61

APPENDIX

The Legislative Package...65

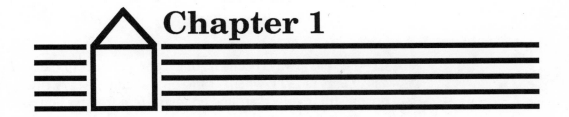

Chapter 1

The Housing Problem

1. A Housing Crisis

Oh give me a home
Where the buffalo roam
Where the deer and the antelope play...

The home has always been one of the cornerstones of the American dream. In 1911, when "Home on the Range" was written, the dream still revolved around an image of a frontier homestead, built by the occupant's own hands. A half century later, after the suburban housing boom that followed World War II, the dream home was a split level with a green lawn in front and a flagstone patio behind. Today, for some, this image may be eclipsed by the fashionable downtown condo.

In any era, the house has represented more than just shelter, more than four walls and a roof. It has coupled shelter with the promise of security, peace, and independence. It has offered refuge, support, and protection.

This dream, in both its bricks-and-mortar and its social aspects, has not always been matched by reality. The crowded coldwater flats of the early 1900s, like the bulldozed slums of the 1950s, showed a not-so-shiny side of the housing picture. And yet, in terms of the degree of homeownership, amenities, or square feet of living space per occupant, U.S. housing standards have improved dramatically over the past half century, rivaling those of any industrialized country. It may seem strange, therefore, to say that this country faces a housing crisis. Nonetheless, the crisis stares us in the face.

Most simply stated, today for more and more Americans, the dream of an adequate, affordable home no longer is attainable. On the contrary, this dream is fading rapidly. In terms of choices, security, neighborhood conditions, and especially **costs**, the housing available to Americans is getting worse.

The starkest evidence of the housing crisis, which has recently captured the attention of the mass media, is the phenomenon of homelessness. For two to three million Americans, home is no more than an overnight shelter, bus station, car, or doorway. **Homelessness in a society as rich as ours should be unacceptable.** It is also, however, only the tip of the iceberg, the most extreme form of a much more pervasive crisis. The following "human interest" stories, backed up by a barrage of disturbing statistics, might appear in any daily paper, any day.

Sally and Jack Novicki have been trying for the past two years to buy a home for themselves and their children in the Baltimore neighborhood where they've lived all their lives. That's where their roots are, where their families live, where they know the shops and schools. But their combined income from Jack's job as a mechanic and Sally's as a part-time nurse simply won't allow them to meet the payments on anything they've seen and liked. They made an offer on one house anyway, hoping to get by with careful budgeting, but when they went to apply for a mortgage the bank officer added up the numbers and turned them down. □

From 1981 through 1986, for the first time in more than 20 years, the nation's homeownership rate fell. Despite some slight improvement in 1987, it remains below the 1980 peak of 66%.

Between 1970 and 1987, the median sales price of existing single-family homes rose from $23,000 to $85,000, while for new homes the median price rose from $23,000 to $104,000. During the same period, mortgage interest rates rose from 8% to a peak of 16% in the early '80s, and have remained at double-digit levels for most of this decade.

The median monthly mortgage payment for first-time homebuyers rose from $122 in 1970 to $572 in 1982, before declining to $451 in 1987 (as falling interest rates more than offset the rising prices). In addition to high monthly costs, high downpayments have also limited homeownership: in 1985, downpayments consumed about half of the typical first-time buyer's annual income, as compared to one-third in 1978.

I n Youngstown, Ohio, James Johnson bought his home a dozen years ago, while he was working steadily in the steel mill. Today, the mill is long gone, and so are the unemployment benefits. He's finally found work as a night watchman. His wife Gloria, who went to community college once the children were old enough, quit school and has found off-and-on waitressing jobs. Nonetheless, they are now two months behind on mortgage payments. The bank threatens to take the house and put it up for sale. □

More than 200,000 homeowners lost their houses to mortgage foreclosure in the deep recession year of 1982. Between 1980 and 1985, the foreclosure rate nearly doubled. In the first three months of 1985, despite several years of economic recovery, 6.2% of all mortgage loans in the U.S. were delinquent (at least thirty days overdue). This figure is the highest since the Mortgage Bankers Association began recording delinquency rates in 1953. In 1987, 5% of all mortgages were still delinquent, primarily due to job loss, falling wages, and divorce (with single mothers unable to meet the monthly payments).

Homeowner displacement, moreover, does not come about only as a result of mortgage foreclosure. Elderly homeowners often find themselves faced with rising property taxes, energy bills, health care costs, and other demands on their strictly limited incomes. The only assets they have are their homes, which often must be put up for sale to convert them from shelter into cash.

Los Angeles resident Sara Garcia and her three children, like a third of American households, rent their home — or rather, their series of homes. In the past five years, they've had to move twice. They lost their first apartment when the landlord doubled the rent. With new skyscrapers towering over the back yard, it was easy to see why. Two years later, their next apartment was converted to a $150,000 condominium, which a young, white, childless couple was eager to buy, to be within walking distance of their jobs. Sara Garcia's newest home — an hour by bus and streetcar from her job — offers cockroaches and crumbling plaster for a rent she can barely manage. □

Each year, about two and a half million Americans — the bulk of them renters — are forced to move because of changes in the housing market. Nearly half of these moves are attributable to increased costs, with the sale of the building accounting for roughly another quarter. For renters, housing costs are rising much faster than incomes: between 1970 and 1983, median rents tripled, while median tenant household incomes only doubled.

Most of the big rent increases have occurred since the late 1970s. During the first half of the '70s, median gross rent as a percentage of median renter income remained fairly steady at about 23-24%. Over the next ten years, rents rose sharply in relation to incomes, with the ratio of median rent to median income increasing to 29-30%, where it remained through 1987.

Since 1983, more than two out of five renter households have not had enough money left, after paying for housing, to meet their needs for food, clothing, and medical care, at even a minimally adequate level. Today, an astonishing one out of five tenant households devote at least one-half their income to housing.

In the competition for scarce affordable rental housing, it is consistently low-income, female-headed, and minority households that fare the worst. Between 1978 and 1985, for instance, median rents for all tenant households increased by 93%. For the very poorest households, however (those with incomes under $3,000), the increase was much higher, 147%.

In terms of condition, in 1983 19% of all renters, 18% of all homeowners, and 25% of all single-parent households (mostly female-headed) lived in housing that was officially classified as inadequate. For Hispanics, the proportion of households in inadequate shelter was about 50% higher than for whites. For blacks, the percentage in inadequate housing was about twice that of whites. Non-white households get the worst housing not just because of lower incomes, but also because of discrimination.

Frank McSherry and Maxine Getz, a working couple, pay $350 a month for their modest garden apartment in suburban Atlanta. Built in 1968 by a private developer, the complex was originally located next to an unsightly abandoned railroad yard. In exchange for the low-interest-rate mortgage loan and substantial tax incentives he received from the federal government, the owner agreed to keep the housing affordable to low- and moderate-income families for twenty years. Now these restrictions have expired, and the developer and his partners have exhausted their tax breaks. The railroad yard has been replaced by a shopping center and is surrounded by new condominium developments, just twenty minutes from downtown on the new interstate highway. Having paid off his federally-insured mortgage, the developer now plans to sell the garden apartments at $80,000 per unit, far beyond the reach of McSherry, Getz, and many other tenants. □

Out of some 600,000 units built under similar federal programs nationwide, 360,000 are located in projects whose occupancy and rent restrictions can terminate over the next ten to fifteen years. Another 300,000 affordable units subsidized under these and other programs could be lost over the same period when their rent subsidy contracts are due to expire. In some rapidly gentrifying neighborhoods, profit-oriented owners are cancelling their subsidy contracts early, while in depressed areas owners are simply exhausting the tax benefits and walking away from their projects. Either way, low- and moderate-income tenants in these privately-owned, publicly-subsidized developments face significant risks of displacement. Once lost from the affordable housing stock, these units are unlikely to be replaced.

The Nguyen family, a couple with four children, has been living for six years in a cramped three-room apartment, all the while expecting a call from the Boston Housing Authority to say that they've finally reached the top of the waiting list. Meanwhile, they can see boarded-up apartments at housing projects in many parts of town. The Authority says it just doesn't have the money to fix them up. So the Nguyens, and the thousands of others on the list, continue to wait, with dwindling hope. □

After 50 years of federal assistance, only 4.2 million subsidized units — less than 5% of all U.S housing — have been produced or provided. Of these, only 1.3 million are public housing units (the rest are privately-owned housing where either the units or the tenants receive some type of government subsidy). In 1982, only one-quarter of an estimated ten million very-low-income American households lived in subsidized units, often the only decent housing they can afford. Today, the existing subsidized housing stock is increasingly threatened due to underfunding, undermaintenance, and the risk of market-rate conversion. And virtually no new subsidized units are being produced: federal budget authority for low-income housing dropped from $32.2 billion in fiscal year 1981 to $8.4 billion in fiscal '87 and '88.

"Even if you don't see it, you can smell it at night. You can hear the fire trucks go by." So said a housing official about the biggest fact of life in a troubled Providence, Rhode Island, neighborhood — arson. The Elmwood neighborhood contains 51 streets of multi-family buildings and Victorian homes converted to apartments as their owners moved to suburbia after World War II. In the '70s, new immigrants and a few returning suburbanites began restoring some of the houses. But in a two-and-a-half year period in the mid-'80s, 29 of these streets suffered at least one intentionally-set fire; one street saw eight houses burn. These were recession years in Providence, when landlords often found no one to rent or sell to. Many owners abandoned their buildings, leaving the property open to vandals. And in some cases, according to the housing official, "I think they (the owners) ended up burning them." □

In Providence as a whole, from 1981 through 1985, there was an arson fire, on average, seven out of every eight days. Nationally, arson displaces tens of thousands of residents each year, and takes over a thousand lives. One of the most common forms — arson for profit — occurs in neighborhoods with high degrees of absentee ownership, abandoned buildings, back taxes owed by owners, and housing code violations; the only way in which owners can still make money on their buildings is to burn them so as to collect insurance settlements. Arson-for-profit also occurs in some neighborhoods undergoing gentrification; here the fires displace existing residents and the insurance money finances luxury rehabilitation.

After ten years of commuting from their cramped St. Louis apartment, Otis Lewis and his family were looking forward to finding a home nearer his job outside the city. Despite their stated preference for living in the mostly white areas convenient to his place of work, all the Lewises were shown were homes in suburban neighborhoods where only other black families lived. When they insisted on seeing homes in white areas, the Lewises were given lukewarm sales pitches, told about difficulties in obtaining financing, and otherwise discouraged from pursuing leads. They

9

settled for a home in a segregated area of a declining suburb, paying what seemed to them an even higher price than the asking price for comparable homes in white neighborhoods. □

Despite passage in 1968 of federal open housing legislation, there has been only a modest decline in residential segregation in the U.S. over the past two decades. While there is considerable movement of black and Hispanic families to the suburbs, this has taken the form of new suburban ghettos, often in towns with declining public services, infrastructure, economic activity, and tax base. "Steering" practices by real estate brokers are a prime contributor to this development, as minority homeseekers are not told about houses in white neighborhoods or are subtly given information that deters them from such areas. "Fair housing audits" in Boston, Denver, Detroit, and other metropolitan areas, using matched pairs of white and minority testers, as well as other studies, have shown clear patterns of discrimination in the treatment of both homebuyers and renters, by realty agents, lenders, insurance companies, and landlords. Such practices often mean that minorities pay more for housing of equivalent quality than do whites. Beyond these institutionalized forms of racism, minority families moving into white neighborhoods still all too frequently can face overt threats, harassment, and violence from neighbors.

2. Causes: The Private Housing Sector

These examples and statistics demonstrate the reality of the housing crisis facing America today: tens of millions of Americans cannot be sure whether their future holds a dream home or a housing nightmare. The prospect of finding a secure home, maintained in good condition, at an affordable price, is far from certain. Government programs, despite great expense, have not prevented the worsening of this situation. A response is urgently needed, but it must be based on a thorough understanding of the problem.

Most simply, the current housing crisis is a crisis of affordability. There is an inexorably growing gap between what housing costs and what people can afford to pay for it. More and more Americans are having to pay ever higher proportions of their income to the landlord or bank in order to house themselves and their families. As the various elements that go to make up housing costs rise faster than the wages and salaries of U.S. households, the situation can only grow worse.

"Housing is a business."

This gap between housing costs and incomes could be overcome in either of two ways: by increasing incomes or by lowering housing costs. To provide everyone with an income sufficient to rent or purchase a decent place to live on the private market, at today's prices, is theoretically possible. We are, after all, a country rich enough to do that. But such massive redistribution of income is hardly likely in the foreseeable future. Therefore, while ways must be found to increase the incomes of households who cannot afford even the most basic shelter expenses, the major challenge today is that of reducing housing costs.

What are the major factors which make housing so expensive? And what can we do, as a society, to reduce the high cost of housing?

Housing is a business. Real estate developers, builders, materials producers, mortgage lenders, investors, speculators, brokers, and landlords build, buy, and sell housing to make a profit. So, naturally, how much housing gets built, where it gets built, how much it costs to build and to buy, and who can afford to live in it depends on what generates the largest profit for these different groups. (Homeowners have two roles: as consumers of shelter and as financial investors; both of these motivations can play a part in how they view their housing decisions. Tenants are housing consumers only, not investors.)

11

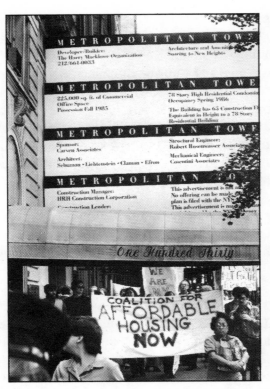

Specifically, the high and rising cost of housing in the marketplace reflects profits made during each stage of its production and use. Land is the fastest rising element in the cost of producing housing, accounting for as much as 25% of the total cost. Interest on construction loans — money developers have to borrow for land, materials, labor, and fees — can add 10% or more to the cost. Developers' overhead is typically 10-15% of the total. Further, most materials used in the construction of housing are produced by giant corporations with few incentives for cost control; construction materials amount to about 25-30% of the final cost. Construction workers' wages are the slowest-rising component, now accounting for only a quarter of the cost of producing a new home.

Once a house or apartment building is produced, its cost to the consumer also reflects the gain made by each owner who resells it for profit in the marketplace. Speculation results in significant increases in the price of both land and housing. The rapid buying and selling of property in search of quick profits is a wasteful use of investment capital; it creates no new housing, but can be extremely damaging, especially to low-income neighborhoods, whose residents can be quickly priced out of the housing market. Most homeowners, too, seek to maximize their profits when they sell their home, resulting in a constant upward spiral of prices. And various "transfer costs" — real estate brokers' commissions, mortgage lenders' fees, attorneys, title search and insurance, etc. — add considerably to the price at each sale.

Additionally, almost every real estate purchase is financed with borrowed funds, adding mortgage interest costs each time. A family purchasing a $100,000 house will typically put down $10,000 or $20,000 in cash, and get a $90,000 or $80,000 30-year mortgage. If interest rates are 10.25%, the total repayment the family will make to the lender on that larger mortgage at the end of thirty years will be in excess of $290,000, over $200,000 of which is interest payments. Use of second mortgages increases these figures greatly.

Mortgage interest rates are not determined by the need or demand for housing, but stem from national and international competition among government and corporate borrowers, and from federal monetary policy. In the early 1980s interest rates soared to nearly three times what they were in the 1950s and early 1960s; despite a dip in the mid-80s, they remain nearly twice as high as they were two decades ago.

"Residential mortgage debt amounts to $2 trillion — more than $8,000 for every adult and child."

Because of runaway housing speculation, residential mortgage debt has grown to be the largest single component of outstanding debt in the U.S. economy. It now amounts to $2 trillion — more than $8,000 for every adult and child. Over the past 40 years, mortgage debt has grown about three to four times as fast as income, making it harder and harder for residents to keep up with their mortgage payments. On homes that have mortgages, repaying that debt takes about two out of every three housing consumption dollars. (Homeowners make the debt payment by writing a monthly check to the bank; for tenants, the debt payment is included in the rent.)

Another problem is that the privately-controlled resources required to build new housing (land, credit, materials, construction equipment, and even construction labor) are not always made available for housing when they are needed. They may be used for other types of production, for speculative investment, or may be kept idle. They are allocated to housing only off-and-on, when it is most profitable for developers, land speculators, materials producers, and mortgage lenders to do so. For example, at the peak of economic booms when business in general is expanding, banks usually cut back on housing loans in favor of more profitable short-term lending to government and corporate borrowers. Similarly, scarce urban land will be used for housing only when higher profits cannot be made from office, retail, or hotel development.

> ## "Government has now officially abandoned the embarrassing task of surveying national housing needs and setting production goals."

Recurring cycles of boom and bust in private housing production, therefore, are even more volatile than the overall business cycle. As a result, the supply of housing is not keeping up with the needs of the growing population. The federal Housing Act of 1968 set a goal of producing 26 million units over a ten-year period, or 2.6 million units a year. Only 21.5 million units were built. The industry's all-time-high production figure came in 1972, with 2.4 million units. By 1981 the annual total was down to 1.1 million units; it rebounded to 1.8 million units by 1986 before starting another descent, down to 1.6 million units in 1987, 1.4 million in 1988. Not surprisingly, the government has now officially abandoned the embarrassing task of surveying national housing needs and setting production goals.

The situation with housing maintenance is similar. Real estate owners and lenders "disinvest" from poor or "high-risk" neighborhoods through undermaintenance, tax delinquency, arson, abandonment, and "redlining" (where banks refuse to lend and insurance companies refuse to insure over whole areas). They put their resources instead into more profitable speculative refinancing and redevelopment of older housing in "upscale" neighborhoods. The same cycle of disinvestment and gentrification also occurs on a regional scale, following the larger movement of private capital from manufacturing to the more profitable service sector, and from Frostbelt to Sunbelt.

Finally, discriminatory practices persist in the housing market in part because they are profitable to certain segments of the industry. For example, "blockbusting" tactics enable real estate speculators to buy cheap and sell dear, while banks convert their old, lower-interest mortgages to higher-yield loans made to new minority homebuyers. Displacement of minority communities through gentrification, redevelopment, or institutional expansion often makes possible new and enhanced opportunities for profit not only in real estate, but also in services; it may also allow cities to compete as tourist and convention centers on the basis of a spanking new (and white) downtown or waterfront.

There is a single, underlying theme which explains our society's current inability to make adequate, affordable housing available to all segments of the population. **Housing is not treated as a necessity of life, to be provided at the highest quality and quantity and the lowest cost for the benefit of those who occupy and use it. Rather, it is treated as a product or commodity, to provide the highest possible profit for those who develop, finance, buy, sell, and manage it.**

3. Causes: Government Actions

Federal government housing policies have not addressed the underlying causes of the housing problem. Rather, they have, on the whole, bridged the gap between housing costs and incomes primarily by reducing risks, guaranteeing profits, and granting tax breaks to the private sector, while providing limited and uneven benefits to housing consumers. That is to say, government has subsidized the high market costs of housing and its components.

15

Over the past several decades, the federal government has directly intervened in the housing market in three main ways. It has assisted the mortgage lending industry by insuring and subsidizing loans to home-owners and private developers. It has allocated direct rental subsidies that guarantee profits to landlords while aiding only a small proportion of needy families. And, most significantly, it has made widespread use of tax deductions and incentives for housing production and ownership which provide windfalls primarily to wealthy homeowners, developers, and investors.

These programs have proven to be both regressive (the bulk of subsidies and tax breaks go to upper-income people) and not cost-effective (they cost far too much for the number of units they provide). They do nothing to change the structure of the private housing industry, and only a small fraction of the money ends up providing decent, affordable housing, while most disappears into a bottomless pit of private greed.

One illustration of this approach is the federally-insured mortgage program offered by private banks after World War II. While the Veterans Administration and the Federal Housing Administration guaranteed and indirectly subsidized banks making low-downpayment, long-term, low-interest mortgage loans for homeownership, allowable tax deductions (for mortgage interest and property taxes) provided additional incentives to homebuyers. These policies made possible the tremendous expansion in single-family suburban housing and the twenty-year growth in homeownership noted above, while also benefitting the finance and real estate development industries.

At the same time, by withholding these loans from the inner city ("redlining"), federal homeownership policies fostered the decline of older low-income and minority neighborhoods. Moreover, they did nothing to contain land or construction costs, or the interest rates on uninsured mortgages.

Today, as government policies still fail to contain these costs, most low-income and many middle-income families find themselves priced out of the market. Inflation and inadequate levels of new construction have driven up the cost of existing homes. High prices, high interest rates, and the prospect of recession and unemployment are making homebuying a risky or impossible venture for all too many families, especially younger households.

Moreover, for many of those lucky enough to already own their homes, the traditional benefits of homeownership are rapidly being undermined. With variable rate mortgages and rising property tax bills, existing homeowners cannot count on cost stability over the long run. And a growing number who live a paycheck or two ahead of the bank risk the loss of their investments — which are also their homes — to foreclosure.

"The tax advantages of homeownership benefit the affluent."

At the same time, the tax advantages of homeownership, far from providing cheaper shelter to the majority, benefit the affluent. Homeowners may deduct mortgage interest and property tax payments from their taxable income, and may defer or exclude capital gains made on the sale of their property. Yet the majority of homeowners don't claim their deduction at all, because they don't earn enough money to warrant itemizing on their tax returns: all told, only one-quarter of American households make use of the homeowner deduction.

In fiscal 1987, according to conservative government estimates, homeowner deductions cost the Treasury nearly $50 billion. The richest one-sixth of the population get two-thirds of the benefits. And what's given away in tax system benefits is nearly four times what the federal government spends directly on housing for the poor and working class (see Table 1).

Not only does the homeowner deduction provide limited benefits to lower- and middle-income homeowners, it also has stimulated housing speculation and displacement of the poor from the inner city. Since the deduction subsidizes primarily the purchase of homes by affluent families, it becomes one more incentive for developers to convert scarce urban rental housing to luxury condominiums.

The one partial exception to the federal government's traditional policy of exclusive support for the private housing industry has been the public housing program. But even public housing was not designed primarily to provide affordable shelter for the poor. The earliest public housing projects were built during World War I for munitions and defense workers to aid the U.S. war production effort. In 1937, public housing became a "pump-priming" program to help get the private economy back on its feet during the Depression. After World War II, more public housing was built, with widespread support, to aid returning veterans.

From the beginning, however, the real estate industry lobbied forcefully to prevent public housing from competing with the interests of private landlords, developers, and mortgage lenders. An "equivalent elimination formula," which required the demolition of one unsafe dwelling unit for every public housing unit created, assured that the overall housing supply would not increase, and that rents and profits in the private housing sector would remain high. Later, in the massive urban renewal and slum clearance programs of the 1950s, public housing became identified with exclusively low-income and increasingly minority populations.

Some of the older public housing developments have been allowed to deteriorate and turn into slums — particularly the high-rise projects built in isolated areas — and much public housing is now "housing of last resort" for the very poor. Racism and lack of concern for the poor have

Table 1

FEDERAL HOUSING SUBSIDIES, DISTRIBUTED BY INCOME, 1988
(estimated)

(households in thousands; subsidies in billions)

Annual Income	Households (1986)		Tax Expenditures for Housing		Federal Outlays for Housing	Total	
	Number	%	Amount	%		Amount	%
Under $10,000	17,130	19.1%	$0.1	0.1%	$10.1	$10.1	15.7%
$10,000 - $20,000	19,157	21.4%	$1.1	2.2%	$2.7	$3.8	5.9%
$20,000 - $30,000	16,350	18.3%	$3.8	7.6%	$1.0	$4.9	7.6%
$30,000 - $40,000	13,167	14.7%	$5.4	10.7%	$0.0	$5.4	8.4%
$40,000 - $50,000	8,667	9.7%	$6.6	13.0%	$0.0	$6.6	10.2%
$50,000 and over	15,007	16.8%	$33.6	66.4%	$0.0	$33.6	52.2%
Total	89,478	100%	$50.6	100%	$13.8	$64.4	100%

Source: Low Income Housing Information Service, *Special Memorandum*, Washington, D.C., April 1988

led to official neglect, chronic underfunding, and often inefficient and overly bureaucratic management. The sad state of some inner-city projects has become a convenient excuse to discredit the concept of public enterprise.

Nonetheless, the majority of the nation's 1.3 million public housing apartments provide decent, well-managed homes for poor families and the elderly, far better than the alternatives offered by slumlords. Evidence of this is most clearly provided by the long waiting lists in most cities — frequently as many families are on the waiting list as the total number of public housing apartments, and, with low turnover, it can take many years before one comes to the head of the line.

"The majority of the nation's 1.3 million public housing apartments provide decent, well-managed homes for poor families and the elderly."

Starting in the 1960s, government policy shifted away from public housing and sought to stimulate private sector involvement in the production of low- and moderate-income rental housing. New programs provided loan guarantees, mortgage subsidies, and, especially, tax incentives that enabled wealthy investors to reduce their personal income tax liability by claiming large artificial depreciation deductions for subsidized projects.

These programs were designed primarily to maximize profits and minimize risks for developers and lenders, at the expense of good-quality construction and long-term affordability. New federal tax policies introduced in 1981 actively promoted the speculative purchase and resale of existing subsidized projects, by allowing the properties to be substantially depreciated over just 5-10 years. As a result, today more than 40% (280,000) of the privately-owned, federally-subsidized units built in the 1960s and 1970s are at risk of being lost through mortgage

default and foreclosure. Another 243,000 units in the more successful projects are ripe for conversion to market-rate housing or office buildings, as their subsidies, rent and occupancy restrictions, and tax benefits expire.

In recent years, the federal government has essentially withdrawn all forms of subsidy, excepting limited tax incentives, for low- and moderate-income housing. Instead, it provides direct rental subsidies to existing landlords on behalf of eligible tenants. Under the Section 8 program, landlords charge prevailing market rents; low-income tenants pay a portion (currently 30%) of their monthly income; and the government subsidizes the rest. Under a recent variation on this theme, the housing voucher program, there is no limit on what the unit can rent for, or on what a family can be forced to pay.

Not surprisingly, these private sector subsidy programs have proved to be extremely costly. In 1982, the direct subsidy cost of a Section 8 apartment was estimated at $4,000-$5,000 a year. More recently, the annual cost of a housing voucher has been estimated at $4,300. And the benefits to tenants are extremely limited. For example, according to a recent study, almost half of all voucher-assisted tenants spend more than 30% of their incomes for rent. About 40% of all Section 8 and voucher tenants are forced to turn back their subsidies because they cannot find affordable apartments — even with the government paying a portion of the rent. In high-cost areas like New York City and Boston, the failure rate is considerably higher.

Conservative critics, who point to the inefficiency of government housing programs, have succeeded in whittling down appropriations year after year, so the programs now serve fewer and fewer families and individuals. The fact is, however, that what has made government policy so wasteful (and therefore vulnerable to attack) has been its commitment to subsidize the ever-increasing cost of private housing ownership, production, and finance. This is why government policies have failed in the past, and why they have provided so little benefit at such great expense.

In place of such wasteful and inadequate approaches, we propose a package of national housing legislation which will for the first time get to the root of the problem and which therefore represents a far more cost-effective solution. The foundations of this program are:

- ■ recognition of housing as a right rather than a commodity;
- ■ elimination of the role of private credit; and
- ■ promotion of social, nonprofit production and ownership of housing units.

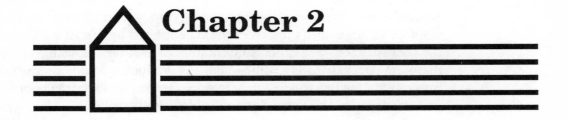

Chapter 2

A Progressive
Housing Program
For America

1. Goals

The Progressive Housing Program for America begins with the assumption that every American household is entitled to adequate shelter at an affordable cost. Every person should be able to find a home in which his or her tenure is secure, without fear of arbitrary displacement; no one's options should be limited by discrimination on the basis of race, gender, or household composition. Housing should therefore be regarded as a **right** — not as a product or commodity which may or may not be available or affordable according to the decisions of private investors and the performance of the marketplace.

As the previous discussion shows, this right has not been secured by the two major forms of housing tenure in our economy: private home-ownership, and rental of apartments from private, profit-oriented owners and developers. It has not been secured by the private production of housing, or by the major mechanism for housing finance — the private mortgage market. Nor has it been adequately secured by government programs, most of which are designed to aid the functioning of these institutions.

The Progressive Housing Program for America therefore proposes the gradual expansion of an alternative form of housing provision and tenure. It seeks to create and promote a nonprofit, non-speculative social sector to develop, own, and manage housing (**social provision**), and it seeks to create full and protected security of tenure for everyone (**protected occupancy**).

Under the proposed Program, government action will be directed toward the following goals, to be defined in more detail below:

1) Expand the amount of housing under some form of social ownership, with residents controlling their housing.

2) Expand the amount of housing produced by socially-oriented developers and increase democratic control over the housing production process and land use.

3) Expand direct public grants for financing housing production, rehabilitation, and ownership, and reduce dependence on privately controlled debt.

4) Provide adequate resources to meet housing needs and allocate housing resources on an equitable basis.

1) *Expand the amount of housing under social ownership, with residents controlling their housing.* Social ownership refers to the operation of housing solely for resident benefit, subject to resident control, with resale for profit prohibited. Under social ownership, the rights of use ordinarily associated with homeownership will be secured and enhanced: security of tenure, privacy, the right to modify one's living space. Only the right to profit in housing will be unavailable. Because socially-owned housing will ultimately be nonprofit with respect to its operation, production, and financing, its cost to occupants will be low, limited to operating and maintenance expenses. Nevertheless, subsidies will be provided where necessary to assure that housing payments reflect true ability to pay.

Social ownership can come about in several complementary ways. One is through conversion of existing privately-owned housing — particularly financially troubled housing, such as apartment houses or owner-occupied homes which are facing the threat of foreclosure. Another is by preserving and expanding social ownership of government-assisted housing that is currently at risk of loss through mortgage default, demolition, or conversion to market-rate use. The third route to social ownership is by way of social production of new housing. Whatever forms social ownership will take, under the Program federal housing funds will be targeted exclusively towards increasing, upgrading, and maintaining the stock of socially-owned and -operated units.

Social owners can range from local government bodies to resident corporations to non-speculative single-family owners. They might be local housing authorities, or other local government entities. They might be community development corporations — locally-based nonprofit development firms which are accountable to the community through

25

election of directors or other means. Similarly, social owners could be community land trusts, neighborhood associations, labor unions, charitable organizations such as settlement houses, or church-based groups. Social owners could also be the residents themselves, individually or collectively, in a nonprofit mutual housing or limited-equity form of tenure* Many of these options could be combined with ownership of the land itself by community land trusts (see p.43), to prevent speculation and make land available for its most socially beneficial (rather than most profitable) use.

2) *Expand the amount of housing produced by socially-oriented developers and increase democratic control over the housing production process and land use.* The Program calls for a substantial increase in federally-supported housing construction and rehabilitation. Not only will such federally-assisted units come under social ownership after they are completed, but a commitment will also be made to increase the number and capability of nonprofit public, community, and worker-owned producers. This includes developers, designers, construction firms, and the suppliers of building materials.

In the short run, however, many aspects of housing production will continue to be carried out by the existing private sector. The Program calls for a production process that is increasingly subject to public and community standards, including democratic control over decisions relating to housing location, design, development, construction, and hiring procedures. An affirmative effort will be made to provide housing

---

*Mutual housing associations are non-profit corporations which develop, own, and operate housing intended to be permanently affordable to the (usually low- or moderate-income) residents. They differ from cooperatives in that, although their boards are resident-controlled, other representatives of the community and public officials also serve, and the associations have an ongoing housing development function, rather than confining their work to a single project. MHA's are very common in Europe

Limited-equity means that when the resident sells, the amount of money that s/he gets is restricted to the amount originally invested as a downpayment or a co-op share, increased by a limited annual percentage. The allowable increase may be a fixed rate such as 6% or 8% a year, or a variable rate such as the rise in the Consumer Price Index.

in forms and locations that address the needs of racial minorities, women, the handicapped, and other groups that continue to suffer widespread discrimination in most housing markets. Resources will also be targeted to develop housing of appropriate size, type, and design in order to provide a supportive living environment for female-headed households and single women.

Additionally, since land is a scarce resource and its rising cost is a significant deterrent to housing development and community planning, the Program will expand the amount of land under democratic rather than market control through government and community land-banking (see p.53) and land trusts (see p.43). Public control over private land will be achieved through a variety of regulatory, tax, and planning measures.

3) *Expand direct public grants for financing housing production, rehabilitation, and ownership and reduce dependence on privately controlled debt.* Even socially-owned housing, if it remains dependent on borrowed money and tax give-aways, is doomed to be expensive to residents and taxpayers, and to remain in short supply. Housing financed through direct grants, on the other hand, will be permanently debt-free, with no mortgages or bonds to repay, and with no need to raise cash through the costly sale of tax shelters to private investors. The federal

government has already used this direct financing method successfully in the construction of tens of thousands of units for military personnel and their families.

This principle will apply not only to new construction, but also to the conversion of existing housing to social ownership, which will be accomplished without adding to the national burden of mortgage debt. As as a growing portion of the existing stock is converted to social ownership, the outstanding debt on these properties will be paid off over time. Prohibition of speculative resale will prevent the build-up of new rounds of debt.

4) *Provide adequate resources to meet housing needs and allocate resources on an equitable basis.* In order to provide decent, affordable housing and viable neighborhoods for all, the level of resources allocated to housing must be substantially increased. A major shift in public spending priorities — most notably away from military spending — will be necessary to provide sufficient funding for the Program. The non-speculative approach to housing embodied in the Program will make it possible to use these funds with much greater cost effectiveness than in the past.

Funds will be targeted especially to benefit households and communities that have been least well served by the private housing market. For example, housing resources will be targeted for the revitalization of existing minority communities, while simultaneously expanding the right of mobility for minority residents by providing increased housing options in other neighborhoods of choice.

To move toward these goals, the Progressive Housing Program for America offers both a comprehensive program and a series of legislative proposals that provide the basis for a new federal housing policy, to be implemented in conjunction with state and local governments and community organizations. The Program seeks to achieve alternative forms of social housing provision and protected occupancy for ever-larger portions of the housing stock, through a series of measures that are designed to:

- ■ preserve affordable rental housing, while promoting the transfer of privately-owned apartment buildings and other rental stock to social ownership;

- ■ prevent homeowner displacement, and foster opportunities for homeownership without speculation;

- ■ retain and enhance the existing stock of public and subsidized housing, under social ownership; and

- ■ produce and finance new and substantially rehabilitated housing for social ownership.

In terms of both need and feasibility, the Program could and should begin today. It is, of course, unrealistic to think that the entire Program will be adopted in the immediate future. Yet, as the housing situation worsens and the limitations of traditional private sector subsidy solutions become more and more apparent, this approach will undoubtedly come to have broad appeal.

The pieces of the legislative package — five proposed Acts addressing different broad components of the housing crisis — are summarized in an Appendix. In the sections that follow, the Program is outlined in detail, in a way that demonstrates concretely how these measures can address the variety of housing problems faced by Americans today. There is no lack of starting points for applying and implementing the program, ranging from protecting homeowners against foreclosure, to salvaging failing government-assisted developments, to strengthening community development corporations and establishing mutual housing associations and community land trusts.

Furthermore, there is no lack of examples to show that, in a necessarily limited way due to lack of resources, many pieces of the Program have already been successfully put to work at the local level. (In fact, a good deal of our thinking has been drawn from such local successes.) Much of this work has been done by local agencies and nonprofit organizations that already provide a model for the social ownership and production entities discussed above. Implementing the national Program would, in many cases, provide these existing groups with the financial resources and technical assistance they need to expand and improve their work. Such pilot examples will be referred to in each of the following sections of this chapter.

"Many pieces of the Program have already been successfully put to work at the local level."

Finally, on the topic of feasibility, it is important to point out that the Program will not necessarily require an increase in the overall federal budget. That is, it will not require additional federal spending or taxation **if** there is a shift in national budget priorities, particularly cuts in the military budget and reform of housing-related tax loopholes. (The costs of the Program are discussed in Chapter 3.)

Likewise, the Program is not a call for yet more centralized federal bureaucracy. The federal government's role will be crucial, but limited: to set standards and minimum requirements, to provide financing, and to assure implementation and compliance.

In order to receive federal funds for housing, economic development, highway and sewer construction, block grants, and other programs which directly and indirectly affect housing, states and localities will have to adopt local housing plans and timetables for the creation of adequate levels of affordable, socially-owned homes. Standards for these units, requirements for regulation of the private housing industry, and mechanisms for using federal funds to increase the stock of social housing will be set forth in the national legislation. However, states and localities themselves will designate the primary planning and implementation agencies that will translate federal legislation into bricks and mortar, homes and neighborhoods, plaster and paint. These local agencies will have broad freedom to design and implement programs that meet the basic requirements in a fashion appropriate to local needs and desires.

What follows is a discussion of how the proposed legislation would address the problems evident in a variety of housing situations. This discussion will demonstrate the paths leading directly from today's housing crisis to the expansion and improvement of a national stock of socially-provided, resident-controlled, affordable housing.

2. Preserving Affordable Rental Housing

The existing stock of privately-owned rental housing provides shelter for 30% of all American households today. It constitutes the bulk of the housing occupied by low- and moderate-income households. The Program seeks to preserve this important national resource, while at the same time improving the situation of many tenants who now face rents they can ill afford, substandard conditions, or fear of eviction or displacement due to rising rents, condo conversions, or demolition of their building.

The Program calls for a series of local regulatory measures which are designed to meet tenants' needs for decent, secure, and affordable housing, consistent with the existing legal requirements that protect landlords' rights to a "reasonable" profit. These regulations are intended, over time, to significantly reduce the potential for speculation in the rental housing market. This will, without a doubt, make rental housing less attractive to many landlords as an investment. Accordingly, the Program also sets forth a number of mechanisms for converting privately-owned units into socially-owned housing.

Localities will be required to enact tenant-protection regulations in order to receive any housing-related federal funds. Conversion of private rental units to social ownership will also provide one means of meeting the targets for socially-owned housing that are established by the local housing plan.

Tenant Protections

Federal funds will be available only to localities that adopt the following basic tenant protection measures. Certain of the protections, however, will go into effect only in the event of a local housing emergency, as determined by local vacancy rates, unemployment rates, and other criteria. Localities will be able to devise their own versions of the required regulations, as long as they meet the following standards:

ANTI-DISCRIMINATION ORDINANCES will be required, to ensure residents maximum freedom of choice in the selection of housing. These will prohibit discrimination on the basis of race, national origin, religion, sex, age, source of income, physical disability, marital status, sexual preference, family size, and presence of children.

LIVABILITY will be ensured by local standards guaranteeing basic conditions for tenant health and safety. Over time, these standards will grow broader, requiring landlords to provide adequate levels of energy efficiency, design of living space, security, and resident services such as child care.

EVICTION CONTROLS will protect tenants from eviction without just cause (such as non-payment of rent, property destruction, or gross violation of community standards). Evictions will not be permitted for luxury rehabilitation or condo conversion unless a compelling public purpose is served and adequate relocation assistance is provided.

RENT CONTROL will be required where a local housing emergency exists. In establishing formulas for rent adjustment, increases will not be permitted to cover the costs of resale or refinancing. All units covered under the ordinance will remain controlled for as long as emergency conditions last, whether or not new tenants move in during this period.

CONDOMINIUM CONVERSION AND DEMOLITION BANS will also be required in a local housing emergency. Condo conversions will be allowed only for limited-equity resident ownership, where at least three-quarters of current residents approve. Demolition may be permitted for a social purpose, with prior one-to-one replacement of units and relocation benefits for tenants.

TENANTS' RIGHTS TO ORGANIZE without reprisal will be guaranteed, and landlords will be required to negotiate in good faith with tenant organizations. In addition, the Program will establish federal standards for the management of private apartment buildings, with respect to building and sanitary code compliance, leases, grievance resolution, non-discrimination, and cooperation with tenant organizations.

LOCAL ANTI-SPECULATION OR DEED TRANSFER TAXES will be required as an indirect measure to hold down rents. These capital gains taxes on profits from the sale of residential buildings will apply to both multi-family and single-family housing. The fewer years a building has been held between sales, the higher the tax rate that will be imposed. These taxes will raise revenues for social housing programs, while discouraging speculation in private housing.

Conversion to Social Housing

Under the Program, localities will be able to meet their social housing goals through a combination of conversion and new construction efforts. One type of conversion will involve privately-owned multi-family apartment buildings, which can be acquired by social owners.

The Program establishes general guidelines for buyout prices and sets forth a variety of mechanisms that can be used to achieve local conversion goals. Localities, as part of their local housing plans, will establish specific conversion targets and mechanisms appropriate to their situations.

The most important source of conversion, initially, will be buildings in trouble — rental housing that might otherwise be lost through abandonment, disinvestment, or arson. Specifically, localities will be encouraged to convert properties that are substandard, tax-delinquent, or facing mortgage foreclosure through the following procedures:

First, in addition to strictly enforcing health, safety, and maintenance standards, localities will be encouraged to condemn and put into receivership buildings that are not brought up to code. ("Receivership" is the power a court has to take control of property away from a negligent landlord and appoint an agent to receive rents and use whatever money is available to make needed repairs.) These buildings can then be transferred to social owners, who will receive grants to perform the needed rehabilitation work. This approach might at first be limited to landlords who have the money to upgrade their buildings but refuse to do so. Owners who cannot afford repairs might be offered rehabilitation grants; in return, they would have to accept strict regulation of rents and evictions, and would have to give a social owner the option to buy the building by a designated future date.

Additionally, localities could expedite foreclosure of properties whose owners have stopped paying property taxes. Ownership of these buildings could then be transferred to a social entity (such as a cooperative or mutual housing association formed by the existing tenants). The social owner would assume any mortgage and pay the back taxes, using a federal grant.

A similar procedure could be used where private owners have defaulted on their mortgages. In this case, the foreclosing bank (or, in some cases, the defaulting owner) would offer local social owners the first option to buy the property with federal funds.

In time, localities will be encouraged to establish a right of first refusal, giving social owners the option to buy any rental property that is offered for sale as long as the price is within federal guidelines.

Eventually, as housing ceases to be a speculative investment and housing prices stop skyrocketing as a result, this option to buy could be used to convert a significant number of multi-family properties to social ownership. Even when buildings haven't been offered for sale, localities will be encouraged to use eminent domain proceedings to acquire them for the purpose of preserving decent, affordable housing. (Eminent domain has been used for years in other types of redevelopment deemed to be in the public interest, most notably in the federal urban renewal program.)

In developing rental housing conversion programs, localities will be required to give priority to buildings occupied primarily by low- and moderate-income households. Once acquired, the properties will either be retained and managed by the locality itself (for instance, by the local housing authority) or transferred to another social owner. The new social owner — whether a government body or a community organization or a resident association formed by the former occupants — will receive federally-funded rehabilitation grants, operating subsidies, and technical assistance as needed. All such properties will remain under permanent social ownership, with speculative resale prohibited.

S everal examples illustrate the potential, even today, for utilizing local regulatory tools to foster the conversion of private rental housing to social ownership. In New York City, about 20,000 units are abandoned each year by private landlords. Most of these units are located in poor neighborhoods, where private landlords and mortgage lenders are increasingly unwilling to invest. Others are found in gentrifying areas, where the City's comprehensive rent, eviction, and condominium conversion control laws prevent landlords from converting their properties to more profitable uses.

Over the years, tenant and community groups have forced the City to take over many of these abandoned properties for non-payment of property taxes. The City currently owns about 10,000 such apartment buildings. Despite poor or nonexistent maintenance, a great many of the apartments are structurally sound and remain occupied by low- and moderate-income tenants. Thousands of other abandoned and tax-

delinquent properties remain legally in the hands of private owners or mortgage holders because the City has not wanted the responsibility of managing and repairing them.

Despite a critical lack of resources, and the City's stated goal of returning these tax-title buildings to private ownership, a number of properties have been successfully rehabilitated and converted to limited-equity tenant cooperatives. For example, under the City's Tenant Interim Lease Program, tenants can form a tenants' association to collect rents and use the funds to repair and manage the building. If successful, they have an option to form a nonprofit cooperative and buy the building from the City for a nominal price. As of January 1, 1985, a total of 130 buildings containing 3,470 units had gone coop in this way, with another 293 buildings operating under tenant management with interim leases.

A second route to social ownership in New York has been for tenants to manage and eventually buy abandoned buildings before the City takes them over — and before they have deteriorated to the point where major repairs are necessary. The Ownership Transfer Project, a demonstration project launched by a private charitable organization, has demonstrated the feasibility of this approach in a small number of buildings in Harlem, Flatbush, the Lower East Side, and other Brooklyn and Manhattan neighborhoods.

In Washington, D.C., some aspects of the Progressive Housing Program for America have been put into practice to protect the city's low- and moderate-income rental housing stock against an onslaught of condominium conversions. The key elements of Washington's approach include its system of rent and eviction controls, its right-of-first-refusal law, and several programs providing financial and technical assistance to limited-equity coops.

Because the City's rent and eviction laws have limited the profitability of rental housing ownership, many D.C. landlords have been eager to sell or convert their buildings or to tear them down for commercial use of the land. However, under the right-of-first-refusal law, these landlords are required to give their tenants forty-five days to organize themselves and make an offer for the building. If the tenants do so, they then have additional time to negotiate, arrange financing, and complete the purchase before the landlord can deal with another buyer. A majority of the tenants in the building must approve the conversion, and elderly residents who don't wish to buy are guaranteed life-tenancy.

"Over 2,000 units in thirty-six buildings had been converted to limited-equity coops in D.C."

This law in itself does not limit speculative ownership; tenants could, for instance, form a standard stock coop, in which share prices (apartment prices) would fluctuate with the private housing market. However, the District of Columbia offers special services and financing to tenants who form limited-equity coops (which, under D.C. law, must limit the annual rate of equity appreciation to 10%). Coops with a majority of low- and moderate-income members are eligible for seed money loans, interim financing, and deferred payment equity loans of up to $20,000 per unit, paid out of Community Development Block Grant and other City funds. As of mid-1986, over 2,000 units in thirty-six buildings had been converted to limited-equity coops under the D.C. program.

Using another approach, Montgomery County, Maryland, has adopted an ordinance which gives the County or its designated housing agency the right to buy any multi-family property offered for sale or conversion, unless a new buyer agrees to maintain the building as rental housing for a specified period. Currently the mandatory rental period is limited to three years, although the County is seeking to extend it. Under this program, the County has purchased two buildings containing eighty-three rental units, using the proceeds of a special 4% tax on condominium conversions. (The conversion tax had generated over $20 million by 1987.)

To be sure, under current conditions all of these local efforts are limited in the scale and scope of what they can accomplish. For example, New York City's increasing reluctance to foreclose on tax-delinquent buildings (and the growing number of landlords who now redeem their tax-title properties for potential redevelopment) has significantly reduced the number of properties available for conversion to limited-equity coops. With rising acquisition prices and limited funds for repairs, District of Columbia tenants are also finding it harder to buy their buildings and run them at affordable monthly costs. Finally, even the most innovative public acquisition programs like Montgomery County's provide limited protection to tenants and are implemented only on an exceptional basis. At the same time, these programs clearly demonstrate how — under the comprehensive framework proposed by the Progressive Housing Program — local regulatory measures can be effectively combined with strategies to promote social ownership.

3. Promoting Affordable Homeownership

It's difficult to deny the attraction of homeownership. Nearly everyone wants the security, control, and sense of community membership it is supposed to bring; there's also the prospect of predictable monthly expenses and the hope of increased property value which can be used to secure improved housing or cash for retirement or other family needs.

Yet many homeowners today find themselves unable to meet their monthly payments or realize the long-term financial gains homeownership was supposed to bring. Most renter families now find homeownership economically impossible.

The Program seeks to protect and enhance the security of existing homeowners, while making the major positive aspects of homeownership available to many other families as well. It establishes a new form of **protected occupancy** that confers the positive benefits of homeownership but eliminates the possibility of speculation, while significantly expanding the stock of social housing to include single-family and other owner-occupied homes.

> **"Most renter families now find homeownership economically impossible."**

In general, the Program will give low- and moderate-income owner-occupants the option to voluntarily transfer ownership of their homes to the social sector. In exchange, homeowners will become "protected occupants," receiving lifetime affordability and security of tenure. Once the owner (or his/her heirs) vacates the house, the unit will be made available to another protected occupant. The unit will not be allowed to be resold for profit on the private market.

Under the Program, federal funds will be available for local programs designed to protect owner-occupied homes and convert them to social ownership:

Where homeowners are threatened with mortgage foreclosure, localities will be able to use federal funds to pay off the mortgage or make tax payments they can no longer afford. In return, legal title to the property will be transferred to a social owner but the resident and his/her heirs will have the right to continue to occupy the house. In cases where the mortgage balance or tax arrearage ends up being much smaller than the value of the house, the local program might also include some cash compensation when the property is transferred, reflecting the owner's equity in the property.

This program will be of particular benefit in communities where plant shutdowns or depressed economic conditions have left large numbers of homeowners on the verge of foreclosure.

For homeowners who can't afford to make needed repairs or improvements, federal funds will be available for home improvement. This assistance will be provided in the form of direct grants, not loans which add to the mortgage debt. In return, the homeowner will agree to transfer legal ownership of the home to a social owner when vacating the property. The amount of the improvement grant will be deducted from any compensation payment for the equity value of the house.

Conversion to social ownership will also be attractive to elderly or other low-income homeowners who are "house-rich" but "cash-poor" — whose homes are their major assets, but who cannot meet sky-rocketing property tax bills or afford necessities other than shelter. Such owners will be able to transfer legal ownership of the home to the social sector, in exchange for both protected occupancy and a lifetime annuity. In this case, the value of the total lifetime payments under the annuity will be deducted from any eventual compensation payment.

Over the longer term, localities will be encouraged to make a standing offer to buy the house of any low- or moderate-income homeowner, not just those who might be willing to transfer their homes because of foreclosure or lack of cash. This broader offer will allow homeowners to sell their houses to a social owner for a reasonable price, while maintaining lifetime tenure subject to a monthly rent based on ability to pay. Buyout prices will be limited by local formulas in accordance with federal standards, and will take into account the gradual elimination of speculation from the housing market and the benefits homeowners will receive in tenure and affordability. One possible formula would be to base the price on what the owner originally paid, adjusted for inflation and improvements, rather than on current market value; the owner would get the difference between the buyout price and

any remaining mortgage balance, with government funds used to pay off the mortgage.

Today's low- and moderate-income homeowners will be the first to benefit from this portion of the Program. But as the stock of social housing grows, more low- and moderate-income households will have the opportunity to become homeowners with all the rights and responsibilities that today's homeowners possess, except for one — profit maximization. When protected occupants eventually vacate their homes, localities will be able to offer these units at low prices to new occupants, who will purchase them subject to limited-equity restrictions. In addition, multi-family buildings acquired by social owners (as described in the previous section) might also be converted to affordable, non-speculative condominiums. These units could be sold to former tenants (aided by grants if needed) on a limited-equity basis.

One program similar to what we have proposed is already operating successfully in Buffalo, New York, under the name of Home Equity Living Plan (HELP). HELP was created in 1981 to preserve housing stock and improve the quality of life of older homeowners by converting their home equity into cash and housing services. The program is sponsored by the City of Buffalo, operated by a nonprofit organization created for this purpose, and financed by federal block grant funds.

Homeowners sell a "future interest" in their house to HELP, but can continue to reside there for life (that is, the owners receive a cash payment in return for naming HELP as the heir to the home upon the resident's death). The cash settlement is calculated using two factors: life expectancy and home value. The homeowner can take the money as a lump sum, or as monthly checks paid out for life. Once the cash settlement is made, HELP performs all major maintenance and pays all property taxes and insurance.

A weakness of the Buffalo program is that, because of lack of funds, the houses do not remain under social ownership. After the resident's death, HELP sells the house on the private market (without limited-equity protections) in order to get funds to buy another house from another elderly resident. Other community homeownership efforts, however, do include the limited-equity model. Among these is the Route 2 Community Housing Corporation (R2CHC) in Los Angeles.

The Route 2 coop grew out of a community battle against the California Department of Transportation (Caltrans), which in the 1960s bought up a large number of mostly single-family homes in the low-income, racially mixed neighborhoods of Echo Park, Silverlake, and East Hollywood. Caltrans planned to destroy more than 500 housing units in order to accommodate a two-and-a-half mile stretch of freeway. In the meantime, it collected rents, though it did little in the way of maintenance.

By 1975, community opposition and rising gas prices had killed the freeway, but Caltrans in the meantime had nearly killed the neighborhood. In the late '70s, however, Caltrans' tenants formed R2CHC to collectively buy and rehabilitate their homes. A federation of five scattered-site limited-equity cooperatives was organized, enabling the residents to become owners of 276 units of housing. The units were bought for a below-market price of $20,000 each, including $10,000 worth of rehabilitation provided by Caltrans. The City of Los Angeles contributed $5,000 per unit in grant funds, to keep costs relatively

NOTICE

The Dellums bill noted on page 66 has been reintroduced in the
101st Congress as H. R. 1122.

affordable. Under the cooperative structure, members' equity is restricted to their original investment plus an increase of no more than 10% a year for thirty years. The cooperatives are managed by a nonprofit subsidiary of R2CHC.

One other form of non-speculative homeownership that has seen increasing use in recent years is the community land trust. Nationwide, about 30 local community land trusts are now in operation, in urban areas from Dallas, Texas to Burlington, Vermont, and in rural areas from the Ozarks to eastern Tennessee to Wisconsin. By mid-1988 they has developed over five hundred units of housing.

> **"Nationwide, about 30 local community land trusts are now in operation."**

The idea of the land trust is that residents may own the building they live in — either on an individual or cooperative basis — but that the land the housing sits on is permanently owned by the land trust. In this way home purchase and mortgage costs can be reduced for the buyer, and speculation on that land can be prevented. Resident owners in turn agree that when they move they will resell their home on a limited-equity basis either directly to the land trust or to another eligible owner.

While community land trusts are designed to ensure long-term affordability and to halt speculation in housing and land, they vary in terms of initial affordability and whom they serve. For example, in the southern Berkshires of western Massachusetts the Community Land Trust has built new one-, two-, and four-family homes, which have been sold to individual owners; a three-bedroom home sells for about $90,000, which is one-half to one-third the average price of private homes in that area.

In Trenton, New Jersey, by contrast, the Latino Community Land Trust (LCLT) has been seeking for years to stop displacement in a neighborhood where most residents have incomes of around $5,000. Starting in 1983, local organizers began working with the Institute for

Community Economics (ICE), a national land trust technical assistance organization, on a plan to acquire a significant number of the units in the Old Trenton neighborhood and remove them from speculative ownership.

While the LCLT was able to buy buildings for as little as $2,000-3,000 per unit, acquisition prices now range from $25,000-30,000 per unit thanks to gentrification promoted by the City. By the Spring of 1988, 95 units had been acquired and transferred to the LCLT. The Land Trust is rehabbing the buildings for $30,000-40,000 per unit, using a below-market interest rate loan provided by ICE as well as some state funds. LCLT is seeking additional private and public funds to further reduce costs. Meanwhile, residents are considering whether the buildings should become limited-equity coops or remain in LCLT ownership as rental housing.

The HELP program, the Route 2 coops, and the land trust movement all embody essential principles of the Progressive Housing Program. However, many of the increasingly popular non-speculative homeownership programs that exist today have significant limitations. One major problem is that the beneficiaries tend to be middle-income, not low- and moderate-income households. The very cheapest units are selling for about $50,000 (and in many areas so-called "affordable" homeownership units cost $80,000-120,000). Mortgage payments, property taxes, insurance, maintenance, and utilities amount to at least $500 a month. No household earning less than $15,000 a year, and very few earning less than $20,000, can afford these units.

Additionally, because most existing homeownership assistance programs have weak resale restrictions, long-term affordability for future residents is not assured. Apart from true limited-equity coops (in which residents upon selling get back only their downpayment or share investment, increased by a limited amount), most single-family or condo ownership programs impose a cap on the total sales price rather than on the homeowner's equity. Thus, an owner making a low downpayment (say, $5,000 on a $50,000 house) can easily double or even quadruple his or her actual investment in five years, even though the sales price increase may be limited to 6-8% a year. Also, even these weak resale restrictions often are not permanent, but limited to the first owner or a specified number of years. Finally, in many programs the resale restrictions are not embodied in deeds or in a permanent title belonging to a land trust, and thus are easily evadable.

4. Protecting Government-Assisted Housing

A third source of low- and moderate-income housing for the social housing stock exists in the numerous, but endangered, apartment projects financed or subsidized by the federal government. These include public housing as well as private and nonprofit developments with federal subsidies tied to the units — together totaling over three million units and constituting a national resource which, once lost, undoubtedly would be prohibitively costly to replace. Today, many of these units are substandard, poorly managed, or threatened with demolition or conversion to luxury housing.

The Program provides a means of converting these troubled projects into secure, livable, affordable, socially-owned housing. To begin with, it sets standards for protecting tenants and upgrading their units. Second, it provides for preservation of public and nonprofit developments for their intended use, and conversion of privately-owned ones to social ownership.

Tenant Protections

In public housing, rents under the Program will be adjusted to more accurately reflect each household's ability to pay. Instead of charging an arbitrary percentage of income (currently 30%), the Program recognizes that what a family can afford to spend on housing depends on the money that's left **after** outlays on taxes and other necessities such as food, health care, and clothing, all of which vary greatly according to family size and other factors. Under one proposed formula, for instance, a four-person family earning $20,000 a year might pay $380 in monthly rent (23% of total income), while a similar family earning $10,000 would pay $130 (16%), and a two-person elderly household with $6,000 would pay $90 (18%). Federal operating subsidies will make up the difference between a project's operating costs and income collected from rents.

Rents in federally-assisted nonprofit projects will also be set according to this type of standard. To make such reduced rents possible for the significant number of financially troubled nonprofit owners, federal funds will be available to cancel defaulted mortgage debt and subsidize operating costs. Privately-owned subsidized projects will also be eligible for such subsidies if they convert to social ownership, as described below.

In addition, housing codes will be strictly enforced, and will gradually be broadened to cover not just basic health and safety but also security, design, energy efficiency, and (where appropriate) child care, elder care, and other social services. Modernization grants will be available to upgrade existing units that are below acceptable standards.

Lease provisions and grievance procedures in all government-assisted developments will be strengthened to enhance tenants' rights. Grounds for eviction (which are already narrower for public housing tenants than for private ones) will be limited to voluntary non-payment of rent, willful destruction of property, or gross violation of community standards. All subsidized housing residents will have the right to participate in collective bargaining over management decisions, including leases, social services, and staffing. Technical assistance and grants will be provided to tenant groups in order to encourage meaningful participation.

Finally, and perhaps most important, managers of government-assisted housing will have to pursue the goal of providing their tenants not only with shelter but with homes. In other words, residents of these projects will as much as possible have all the benefits, other than profit, associated with owner-occupied housing today; these include security, freedom of choice, resident control, and pride of ownership.

> **"Residents will have all the benefits, other than profit, associated with owner-occupied housing: security, freedom of choice, resident control, and pride of ownership."**

Therefore, firms or groups seeking contracts to manage government-assisted housing will have to apply to localities for licensing. Licensing authorities will look for commitment to tenant participation, willingness to provide services that improve the quality of life, and proven ability to carry out sound financial management. The Program will provide funds to encourage the development of alternative forms of management for social housing. Wherever possible, preference will be given to nonprofit organizations whose primary concern is to provide services rather to make a profit. Such "social management" firms will include management entities formed by the tenants themselves.

Expanding Social Ownership

In addition to these tenant protection measures, the Program includes requirements to make sure that existing government-assisted housing is preserved for those who need it most — and to encourage its conversion to social housing in the fullest sense.

First, **all** units in existing subsidized developments will be permanently maintained as low- and moderate-income housing. However, existing tenants whose incomes rise will not be forced out of their units; they will be able to stay, paying a higher rent determined by the ability-to-pay formula. Removal of units from the subsidized housing stock (through demolition, conversion to nonresidential use, or conversion to market-rent housing) will be generally prohibited; in the case of any exceptions granted for compelling public purposes, one-to-one replacement and relocation assistance will be required. Sale from a social owner to a private one will be prohibited as well. (However, within the social sector, a housing authority could transfer ownership to a cooperative or other nonprofit organization so long as the transfer does not harm current residents.)

Privately-owned, government-assisted projects will be converted to social ownership whenever possible. When these projects are offered for sale, the Program will give a right of first refusal to the tenants, and then to other prospective social owners. Direct federal grants will help the new social owners with purchase, rehabilitation, and technical assistance, and operating subsidies will be provided as needed. The backlog of repair costs and debt burdens will be eliminated, reducing future costs to a manageable level. (Federal regulations will limit the allowable purchase grant; in any case, permanently restricting the units to low- and moderate-income occupancy will keep acquisition prices relatively low.)

The Program will offer private owners incentives to cooperate in this kind of conversion. Government-subsidized developers in good standing will be eligible for mortgage debt writedowns (cancellations), rehabilitation grants, and operating subsidies, in return for an agreement to eventually sell the properties to the tenants or another social owner. In order to ensure that owners who have not lived up to their responsibilities yield control of subsidized buildings, these incentives will be coupled with strict enforcement of existing federal regulatory agreements. Private owners who have defaulted on their mortgages or failed to meet existing federal standards for maintenance and management will face foreclosure. If they do not then agree to transfer title to a social owner, the government will foreclose and sell the property to a social owner.

Several pilot examples of preservation and/or conversion of subsidized projects, achieved through tenant activism with support from local government and nonprofit institutions, suggest the feasibility of this approach.

In Boston, a number of large public housing projects have been substantially redesigned, upgraded, and preserved as public housing. In one instance, the 648-unit Fidelis Way development on a choice hilltop location had been mismanaged and allowed to decay to the point where fewer than half the units were occupied. The remaining residents, fearing that the property would be sold for luxury redevelopment, took strong political and legal action that resulted in conversion from a state-aided to a federally-aided project. Federal funds were then used to accomplish very substantial redesign and rehabilitation. All residents were guaranteed the right to stay, but redevelopment did eliminate 200 units. Additionally, because of the Boston Housing Authority's limited development and management capabilities, both the rehabilitation and the ongoing management of Fidelis Way have been contracted out to private companies; however, tenants have negotiated strong contractual rights to oversee these operations.

Across town, Boston's D Street project is also being redesigned and preserved as public housing, in this case with state funds and a smaller loss of units. At nearby Columbia Point, however, the city's Housing Authority has sold a 1,500-unit project to a private developer for conversion to "mixed income" housing, with an obligation to permanently maintain only 400 low-income units. Despite "guarantees" that they would be rehoused, many of the roughly 350 low-income families who have survived in the long-neglected project cannot meet the stringent management standards imposed by the new private owner.

Elsewhere in Boston, at Methunion Manor, a 150-unit federally-subsidized project located in the rapidly gentrifying South End neighborhood, the tenants succeeded in blocking a series of foreclosure sales which could have resulted in their displacement. The federal government then agreed to take over Methunion and sell it to the residents as a limited-equity cooperative for a nominal price (less than $100 per unit). In addition to repairs paid for by the government, the cooperative financed additional improvements through a loan from the National

Cooperative Bank and resident downpayments of $750 to $1,080 per unit.

Methunion Manor now has the potential for long-term viability. Mortgage debt service has been reduced to $56 per unit per month. The coop's deed obligates it to maintain the project as affordable housing for at least thirty years, to seek new rental subsidies when necessary, and to offer a right of first refusal (in the case of sale) to a local charitable corporation.

Across the continent, at Saratoga Court, a twenty-unit elderly housing complex located in the wealthy bedroom community of Saratoga, California, the developer decided to cancel his rental subsidy contract early to take advantage of the local real estate boom. In less than five years, the market value of the project had grown to more than twice its original cost. The tenants organized and, with the help of the city government, negotiated a sale to the Mid-Peninsula Coalition Housing Fund, a Palo Alto-based nonprofit development corporation. To finance the acquisition price of close to $1 million, Mid-Peninsula arranged to take over the existing federally-subsidized mortgage, secured Community Development Block Grant funds from the city and county, and sold tax shelter benefits to private investors through a social investment fund.

Saratoga Court's ownership structure now includes some long-term affordability safeguards. The subsidy contract has been extended for the maximum fifteen-year term; the project must be maintained as low-income housing for the term of this contract; and then another nonprofit entity has an option to buy. In addition, the project is now managed by Mid-Peninsula's nonprofit management company.

Other community-based groups have successfully managed government-subsidized housing. In the Mount Auburn neighborhood of Cincinnati, a community organization formed a nonprofit development arm to renovate townhouses-turned-apartments that were falling victim to deterioration and abandonment. The Good Housing Foundation — controlled by a board made up predominantly of low-income, black, female heads of household — originally hired a large, conventional for-profit management company to run the restored, federally-subsidized development. However, when the board became dissatisfied with the low level of care and attention provided by the managers, its members decided to set up their own firm, Mount Auburn Management, which now handles upkeep, tenant selection, rent collection and finances, planning, and other services for 550 housing units and 25 commercial units, including a grocery store and health center.

"Community-based groups have successfully managed government-subsidized housing."

Of the current staff of eighteen management, clerical, and maintenance personnel about half are building residents. In addition, tenants make up the Foundation board which sets overall policy, form a majority on the tenant screening committee, and organized into tenant associations in each building. The management firm's first priority is regular preventive maintenance; the maintenance crew is expected to have any vacated units ready for new occupants within three days. Mount Auburn Management also provides management services to a neighboring community development group; more important, unlike private management firms, it has agreed to work itself out of a job by training the community development staff to take over the tasks themselves.

These examples illustrate the potential for preserving and upgrading existing subsidized housing under new forms of social ownership. However, they also demonstrate the need for a more comprehensive approach. Today, for every subsidized project like Fidelis Way or Methunion Manor that tenants succeed in saving, many more are being lost through deterioration, demolition, or conversion to market-rate housing. Tenant and nonprofit ownership or management of subsidized housing is the rare exception rather than the norm. Additionally, without mechanisms to reduce the acquisition value of projects like Saratoga Court, few nonprofit groups will have the money to purchase them. Finally, as long as nonprofit sponsors are forced to rely on traditional tax-shelter financing mechanisms, permanent affordability cannot be guaranteed. The alternative approach provided by the Program not only will mandate and support the kinds of positive local efforts illustrated by these examples, but also will make it possible to preserve existing subsidized units as decent affordable housing on a **permanent** basis.

5. Producing and Financing Affordable Housing

Production

An important prerequisite for non-speculative, affordable housing is adequate supply. The protection and conversion programs discussed so far address the issue of supply by ensuring that troubled low- and moderate-income housing is not left vacant or uninhabitable, demolished, or redirected to speculative purposes. There remains, however, the task of maintaining a steady flow of new construction. As localities plan how to meet the goals for social units set in their local housing plans, they will set appropriate targets for construction as well as for the various types of conversion. The balance between construction and conversion/rehabilitation will depend on the housing stock, needs, and population trends of the state, city, or town.

Under the Program, new housing construction will be directed toward the goal of meeting community needs and promoting social ownership, and will be funded through direct federal grants. This approach will assure affordability and also avoid the cycles of boom and bust that have plagued the private housing industry. Social sector units will be the **only** new housing to receive federal financial assistance.

Localities will use federal funds to buy land suitable for housing development, as that land becomes available. This land will be held by public agencies or community land trusts in anticipation of future development, rather than being acquired parcel by parcel only as needed. Such land-banking will, in the long run, significantly reduce the cost of building new homes, because it will interrupt the cycle of speculative buying and selling which drives up the price of land.

> **"Direct federal construction grants will assure affordability and avoid the boom and bust cycles that have plagued the housing industry."**

In new production, as well as in the rehabilitation of housing, the Program seeks to steer development, design, and construction contracts toward nonprofit groups, whose principal concern is to provide housing rather than to maximize profit. Initially, much of the work will no doubt be done by private, for-profit companies working under contract to a social owner. In any subcontracting, however, the private developer will be required to give priority to competent public, nonprofit, or cooperative firms when they can be found (for example, community-based designers, nonprofit materials suppliers, construction craft cooperatives, etc.). Technical assistance funds will be available to foster the growth of a truly social sector of housing production.

In addition, developers (whether private or social) will be required to involve local residents in planning and monitoring new housing construction. Design will have to meet federal standards for livability with respect to site, apartment size and layout, building materials, provision of social services, and other factors. Developers will also be required to comply with federally-mandated affirmative action criteria in the hiring and training of minority and female employees. Completed housing, particularly multi-family housing, will have to be managed and maintained according to strict standards of resident protection — whenever possible, by social management firms.

Some aspects of the proposed social production program are already well established. Across the country, nonprofit housing organizations (most of them community-based) are responsible for a growing share of low- and moderate-income housing production. In Massachusetts, about seventy-five nonprofit sponsors have created 7,000 affordable housing units since 1975, with another 2,000 units in the pipeline. Total rehabilitation and construction by New York City neighborhood groups is estimated at 3,000 units annually. San Francisco's nonprofit developers, with a later start than many East Coast counterparts and an extremely speculative housing market, have produced 2,000 to 3,000 affordable units in recent years. The Chicago Rehab Network has more than 1,000 units in production, and Cleveland nonprofits are providing 200-400 units annually in a market where little new housing investment is taking place.

In recent years, as housing production costs have risen and federal subsidy resources have dwindled, local nonprofit sponsors have been forced to develop complex ownership and financing strategies that often rely on larger nonprofit intermediaries. For example, nonprofit housing production in Boston is currently dominated by the Boston Housing Partnership, a new citywide nonprofit representing public, private, and neighborhood interests, which aggregates financing and subsidies for use by local sponsors. At the national level, nonprofit organizations such as the Local Initiatives Support Corporation, the Enterprise Foundation, and the Neighborhood Reinvestment Corporation play an increasing role in structuring and financing community-based projects.

There are also clear (if limited) examples of nonprofit groups undertaking other aspects of housing production. In Boston, several construction unions formed the Bricklayers and Laborers Nonprofit Housing Company to demonstrate that housing for working-class consumers can be provided by a nonprofit builder paying union wages. In their initial project, 17 attractive brick, bow-front townhouses were sold as resale-restricted condominiums for approximately $70,000 each, about half the market price for comparable units in the neighborhood. Cost savings were achieved by eliminating development fees, by pur-

chasing the land (a former school site) from the City for one dollar, and by using union pension fund deposits to obtain a below-market interest rate construction loan. The Bricklayers are currently developing another 200 affordable units in similar neighborhoods across the city.

In addition, the Boston Building Materials Cooperative sells an annual total of $350,000 worth of construction supplies to 650 members. Members are local homeowners who can't afford to hire contractors to make repairs. The coop is nonprofit, selling discount materials as well as providing free advice and workshop space. Its staff also provides on-site consulting, charging hourly fees according to an income-based sliding scale.

While these examples demonstrate the potential for social production, their limitations under current conditions are readily apparent. Nonprofit sponsors today develop only a fraction of all new units, and they find it difficult to compete with private developers for sites and subsidies. The innovative construction efforts of the Boston Bricklayers Union and the Boston Building Materials Cooperative represent isolated examples in industries which are privately dominated and controlled. Finally, as long as nonprofit developers remain dependent on banks and other traditional private financing sources, it will remain difficult for them to significantly reduce production costs. The proposed Program will allow these social entities to do their work on a much larger — and continually expanding — scale, and to produce housing which is permanently affordable to low- and moderate-income residents.

Finance

All conversion, construction, and rehabilitation of social housing under the Program will be financed by direct federal capital grants. This will be considerably more cost-effective than the present system of private mortgage guarantees and tax subsidies which primarily benefit lenders and wealthy investors. Direct grants will remove the substantial capital cost component of rents (the portion going toward paying off the mortgage). Housing costs in the social sector will be further lowered by other provisions of the Program that eliminate profits from operations and speculative resale.

Nonetheless, there will still be households who cannot afford the monthly cost of managing and operating housing in the social sector. (Even without debt, housing consumers have to pay for heat and electricity, water, repairs and maintenance, insurance, and property taxes, expenses that can easily exceed what a low-income family can afford.) Therefore the federal government will also provide annual subsidies to operate the housing in order to assure that rents or limited-equity ownership expenses do not exceed residents' ability to pay. Operating subsidies targeted to socially-owned and -produced housing will be considerably more cost-effective than current subsidy programs that bridge the gap between incomes and private market rents.

Standards for determining which households deserve subsidies, and how much, will be set at the federal level. In place of rigid percentage-of-income formulas, the Program will recognize that different sizes and types of families have different amounts of non-shelter expenses that must be taken into account — such as expenses for medical and child care. Over time, as the effects of the Program continue to reduce housing costs, subsidy formulas will be readjusted to allow higher deductions for these expenses, and thus a higher standard of living.

While direct grants represent a radical departure from current housing finance methods, which rely heavily on private credit, the impediments to such a shift are largely ideological, rather than economic.

In fact, the Program's feasibility is demonstrated by a number of precedents.

The best-known example is public housing, of which today there are some 1.3 million units. Although public housing has traditionally been financed through tax-exempt bonds sold to private investors, this debt is paid off over time by the federal government, removing the burden of capital costs from the housing and from the tenants' rents. In addition, since the 1960s the government has subsidized public housing's operating costs, and charged rents as a percentage of household income (currently 30%). While this arbitrary rent formula does not reflect what different types of families can truly afford to pay, public housing units represent the most affordable housing in the United States today. Unlike other forms of subsidized housing, they are also debt-free and owned and operated exclusively on a nonprofit basis, with opportunities for resale strictly limited (although not entirely prohibited).

An alternative method of capital grant financing involving direct government spending comes from the military budget, a major source of potential funds for the Program. In communities where the private housing stock is inadequate, the Defense Department has built some 450,000 units of off-base family housing for armed forces personnel. Construction of a substantial portion of these units, maintenance, and modernization have all been accomplished by means of direct allocations from Congressional appropriations to the Pentagon budget.

Other applications of this direct financing model can be found at the local level. In the mid-'70s, the redevelopment and housing authority of Portsmouth, Virginia, made use of federal Community Development funds to directly finance construction of forty-eight apartments in order to relocate families displaced by other redevelopment activities. The authority concluded this was the only way make the project self-sufficient at rents the relocated households could afford. A similar example, involving the use of local public funds to directly finance the acquisition of apartments threatened with condominium conversion, is provided by Montgomery County, Maryland, as described in Section 2 of this chapter.

Finally, the Baltimore Mutual Housing Association provides an innovative model which combines elements of both the social production and public financing aspects of the Program. Established in 1982 through the Neighborhood Reinvestment Corporation, the Association has developed forty-nine townhouse units on a ten-acre site in the Govans neighborhood of Baltimore. The units are owned by a nonprofit corporation controlled by current and prospective residents; other community representatives also serve on the board. About two-thirds of the $7 million development budget has come from direct grants provided by a variety of public and private sources. These include Urban Development Action Grants, Community Development Block Grants, corporate contributions, and a special federal appropriation secured by the Neighborhood Reinvestment Corporation for its mutual housing demonstration program.

Because of these financing arrangements, the monthly costs of the Baltimore units are low, ranging from $270 to $380. Permanent affordability is further assured by "mutual ownership," which requires no equity investment by members, and pays no return on equity if and when they move out. (Residents do pay an initial membership fee of $2,100 to $2,500 which is refunded when they vacate their units.) Surplus monthly revenues, if any, will be used to help finance the construction of additional units.

Funded by a second federal capital grant, the mutual housing demonstration has now been extended to New York City, where sixty vacant tenement units on the Lower East Side will be rehabilitated. The Neighborhood Reinvestment Corporation plans to initiate similar projects in at least five other cities, but these may not be debt-free because additional capital grant funding has so far proved difficult to obtain.

The principal limitation of these social financing examples is their exceptional nature. Public housing, chronically struggling for survival, has long been eclipsed by subsidy programs to the private sector utilizing private credit and capital. The success of the military housing program is, of course, embedded in the politics of the military budget. The Virginia case, while revealing great local initiative, took place only after unsuccessful attempts to get a conventionally-financed private development on the site, and with the reluctant approval of the federal government.

Finally, the Neighborhood Reinvestment Corporation's mutual housing demonstration, which in many ways most closely exemplifies the basic principles of the Program, so far has proved difficult to repeat because of the scarcity of direct grant funding. Under the proposed Program, the direct financing approach, which today is used reluctantly or with great difficulty, would become the "first resort" strategy both for public and nonprofit developers.

6. Conclusion

The goal of providing every American with decent, affordable housing is achievable. The Progressive Housing Program for America is based on common-sense. It uses taxpayers' dollars wisely and cost-effectively to assure all Americans the right to homes they can afford, can live in with reasonable comfort, can count on staying in, and can control.

This analysis outlines the source of our nation's housing problem, as well as a solution: the creation of housing for use rather than profit, the replacement of private housing ownership, production, and finance with a system of social provision and protected occupancy. A number of mechanisms have been proposed, in four main categories, for getting from today's problem to tomorrow's solution. In each case existing pilot projects have been identified, mostly undertaken on a small scale, which begin to demonstrate the feasibility of the approach proposed here.

These projects are of course tiny in comparison to the dimensions of the national problem. They have also been limited by the available forms of financing, ownership, and control. The solution is not to reproduce these initiatives, even on a much larger scale, but to undertake a national effort which puts their strengths together as parts of a comprehensive and integrated programmatic solution. This approach will require federal leadership and federal funding, as well as the capacity for decentralized implementation based on local resources and needs.

The Program will cost a lot at first — possibly $29 - $87 billion in its first year (see Chapter 3 for details) But it will save even more over the long term. These funds are being called for at a time when the federal government has been running rapidly away from any commitment to low- and moderate-income housing at all. One dramatic statement of the Reagan Administration's priorities is that while in 1981 the ratio of federal spending on the military to spending on housing was 7:1, during Reagan's years that ratio rose to 43:1.

But the "housing climate" is right for a radical change. As of this writing (late 1988), there is clear evidence of new and serious Congressional interest in meaningful federal legislation to meet the nation's housing affordability crisis. The housing movement, at the national and state/local levels, also is taking on renewed energy, through tenant and neighborhood organizations, city- and statewide coalitions, community development corporations, anti-redlining efforts, and the various groups advocating on behalf of the homeless. Public opinion polls commissioned by the National Housing Institute and other organizations show widespread support for a true national housing effort to provide "a decent home and suitable living environment for every American family" (the National Housing Goal set by Congress in 1949), and to raise taxes, if necessary, in order to pay for such a program. As this grassroots movement expands, and as the realities of the housing crisis increase and become more evident, political leaders will be forced to respond. The way to move forward is to articulate and work for a bold new approach that is both feasible and cost-effective. The Progressive Housing Program for America is intended to stimulate that effort.

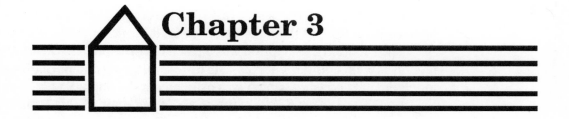

Chapter 3

First-Year
Program Costs

First-Year Program Costs

The following Table summarizes three possible First-Year Options for beginning to implement the Program. Per-unit costs for the major components of the Program have been estimated, along with a suggested possible mix of these components which would be feasible at each of the three levels of total Program cost.

The Medium Cost Option was chosen to correspond to the level of federal tax expenditures (taxes lost to federal government due to tax loopholes) for housing, which was estimated to be about $54 billion in FY1988. The Lower Cost Option is about one-half of this total, and represents a minimum level for beginning to implement each major component of the Program. The Higher Cost Option reflects a substantially greater commitment to new construction and rehabilitation, the elements of the Program with higher per-unit costs; it likely represents the maximum production level which could be achieved administratively and physically in the first year.

Beyond the first year, Program costs similarly will depend on political choices as to the level of Program activity. In time, there will be a leveling off of capital grants for rehabilitation as the existing substandard stock is brought up to par, and a steady decrease in government funds needed to pay off existing mortgages on housing brought into the social housing sector as these mortgages are retired.

The Program addresses a serious misallocation of private and public resources devoted to housing, stemming from the dominance of speculative over productive investment and the reliance on private credit to finance housing. Nonetheless, even though it is much more cost-effective as a way of directing the society's resources toward meeting the society's housing needs, the Program will cost the federal government lots of money. Where will this money be found?

The answer is that there is no shortage of resources for housing or any other reasonable social objective. The Medium Cost Option, for instance, would cost less than 5% of FY1988 federal budget, or a little over 1% of GNP. Yet tapping these resources will require substantial tax reform (including both greater equity and increased revenues to close the deficit) and also a shift in national spending priorities away from the military budget. The Higher Cost Option amounts to only one-quarter of the Pentagon budget.

Table 2

A PROGRESSIVE HOUSING PROGRAM FOR AMERICA
FIRST-YEAR OPTIONS

	Cost/ Unit (thou.)	Lower Cost #units (thou.)	$ (bill.)	Medium Cost #units (thou.)	$ (bill.)	Higher Cost #units (thou.)	$ (bill.)
Conversion of Private Rental Units (a)	$35	100	$3.5	160	$5.6	200	$7.0
Conversion of Homeowner Units (b)	$50	100	$5.0	160	$8.0	200	$10.0
Conversion and Modernization of Existing Subsidized Units (c)	—	430	$4.8	580	$6.3	880	$9.3
Rehabilitation of Converted Units (d)	$20	100	$2.0	400	$8.0	600	$12.0
New Construction for Social Ownership (e)	$60	50	$3.0	200	$12.0	500	$30.0
Operating Subsidies for Social Housing (f)	$2	5000	$10.0	6500	$13.0	8000	$16.0
Administration (g)			$1.2		$2.0		$3.5
TOTAL			$29.5		$54.9		$87.8

Notes to Table 2

(a) Assumes full payment of negotiated price in year acquired; per unit costs from Chester Hartman and Michael Stone, "A Socialist Housing Alternative for the United States." In Rachel Bratt, Chester Hartman, and Ann Meyerson (eds.) *Critical Perspectives on Housing*. Philadelphia: Temple University Press, 1986.

(b) Assumes full payment at time of acquisition for mortgage balance and negotiated equity.

(c) Assumes cost of $1.3 billion to retire debt on 80,000 HUD-held units; $500 million for equity compensation to owners of 100,000 units with expiring use restrictions; balance for modernization and modest rehab of public and other subsidized projects at about $10,000 per unit. (See Emily Achtenberg, "Subsidized Housing at Risk: The Social Costs of Private Ownership." In Sara Rosenberry and Chester Hartman (eds.) *Housing Issues of the 1990s*. New York: Praeger, 1989.)

(d) Rehabilitation cost only; acquisition cost is included under the conversion element of the Program. Cost per unit is based on data from various rehabilitation projects.

(e) Per unit cost is based on construction spending figures for 1984, adding in land and subtracting construction financing costs (financing through direct grants eliminates construction financing costs). (See the Hartman-Stone article cited in note a) for sources and methods.)

(f) Covers operating expenses only, as debt service is included under the conversion portion of the Program; derived from 1983 operating costs data, adjusted to 1985, and applying Stone's affordability scale. (See the Hartman-Stone article cited in note a) for sources and methods.)

(g) Conservative estimate.

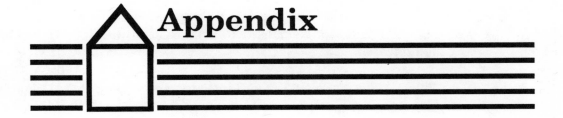

Appendix

The Legislative
Package

The Legislative Package

The Progressive Housing Program for America has been introduced in the House by Congressman Ronald Dellums (D-CA) as H.R. 4727, A Bill to Provide an Affordable, Secure and Decent Home and Suitable Living Environment for Every American Family... (When reintroduced in the 101st Congress, it will be given a new number.) The Act contains five sections, each with its own funding authorization.

Title 1 - <u>The National Tenant Protection and Private Rental Housing Conversion Act</u>

This section establishes standards that limit the control exercised by private landlords and managers over the terms and conditions of residential tenancy in the private market. It sets forth a series of mechanisms and procedures to facilitate the phased conversion of a significant portion of the private rental housing stock to various forms of social ownership. It enables localities to adopt such measures, appropriate to their needs, as one means of meeting federally-mandated goals for provision of affordable social housing.

Title II - <u>The National Homeowner Protection Act</u>

This section seeks to facilitate the positive aspects of conventional homeownership (security, control, cost stability, ties to community) while eliminating the negative ones (unavailability to many low- and moderate-income persons, risk of mortgage and tax foreclosure, incentives to speculation). Toward this end, the Act requires localities to encourage the voluntary transfer of private homes to the social sector in exchange for enhanced affordability, improved maintenance, and increased security of tenure (protected occupancy). Non-speculative, limited-equity homeownership, either cooperative or individual, is promoted as an alternative tenure form. The Act establishes programs for the rehabilitation and social ownership of existing single-family homes, again as one means for localities to meet their federally-mandated housing goals.

Title III - <u>The Subsidized Housing Preservation Act</u>
This section seeks to improve the affordability and livability of the subsidized housing stock, assure security of tenure, and increase resident control for current and future low- and moderate-income tenants. It also provides mechanisms to assure the permanent retention of existing subsidized units, enhance existing public and nonprofit ownership, and to facilitate conversion of privately-owned subsidized units to forms of non-speculative social ownership.

Title IV - <u>The Social Housing Production and Financing Act</u>
This section sets national goals and provides federal assistance for the production of new housing and rehabilitation of existing housing that will be owned and financed exclusively within the social sector. The Act stipulates that the process by which new and rehabilitated housing is developed will be subject to public and community control, with production increasingly steered toward nonprofit and public developers. It further provides that social housing production and conversion will be financed exclusively by means of direct federal capital grants. These grants will be supplemented by a system of universal operating subsidies to bridge the gap between what tenants in the social sector can afford to pay and the ongoing cost of operating the housing.

Title V - <u>Federally-Mandated Local Housing Programs</u>
This section details the roles of federal, state, and local governments in implementing the Program set forth in the preceding Acts.
The role of the **federal government** is two-fold: to establish general guidelines and minimum requirements, and to provide the financial and technical resources for localities to meet or exceed these guidelines and requirements. Federal funds for housing, highway, and sewer construction, economic development, Community Development Block Grants, and other federal programs that directly and indirectly impact housing will be restricted to states and localities that affirmatively satisfy their housing responsibilities. Administration of the Program elements is to be as decentralized as possible.

Primary responsibility for enforcing compliance will rest with **state governments,** each of which will designate an agency (presumably an existing housing or planning agency) to carry out this role. State agencies will pass on federal funds to localities, and will monitor local compliance with Program requirements. States will also establish state, county, or regional housing authorities to carry out housing activities in localities which are too small, inexperienced, or otherwise unable or unwilling to design and implement housing plans themselves.

To be eligible for federal funds, **localities** will be required to adopt and carry out local housing plans providing for production and rehabilitation of socially-owned housing, conversion of existing units from private to social ownership, preservation and upgrading of existing subsidized housing through new forms of social ownership, and regulation to protect tenants in private and government-assisted rental housing. Local governments will be required to assess the housing needs of all economic and racial groups in the community, and to set targets and schedules for meeting these needs. If a local government does not participate in the Program, local nonprofit agencies will be able to receive funds for Program activities directly from the state housing authority.

Photo Credits

Cover

Blueprints: Michael Mostoller & Fred Travisano, Architects

Chapter 1

p. 5   Mark Jahr/*City Limits*

p. 8   Bill Goidell/*City Limits*

p. 12   George Cohen/*City Limits*

p. 16   Chip Cliffe

p. 21   Ted Goff/*Shelterforce*

Chapter 2

p. 27   David L. Brown

p. 32   Mark Hoffman/City Life/Vida Urbana

p. 36   Fred Ohringer/Urban Homesteading Assistance Board

p. 41   *City Limits*

p. 44   Trust for Public Land

p. 50   Christopher Brown/Mass. Community Economic
        Development Assistance Corporation (CEDAC)

p. 55   Photographer: © Steve Rosenthal, 1986
        Developer: Bricklayers and Laborers Non-Profit
                     Housing Co., Boston, MA
        Architect: William Rawn Associates